Graeagle

History of Mohawk Valley

Including

Clairville and Johnsville

C. L. Neely

Originally published in 1990 by Chicken Scratch Studio

Behind Every Hero
Copyright ©1990 C. L. Neely

2nd printing

All rights reserved. No part of this publication can be reproduced, stored in a retrieval system, or transmitted in any form or by any means—electronic, mechanical, photocopy, recording or any other—except that copying permitted by U. S. Copyright Law, Section 107, "fair use" in teaching or research, or for brief quotations in printed reviews, without permission in writing from C. L. Neely.

For information: carrien2u@yahoo.com

Photos are by author, Bertha Miller, Ed White Collection, and the author.

Special Thanks
To
Larry Neely
For encouragement
and help.

Introduction

This small history was first printed in 1990, and although the history does not change, there are references to the current situation of different areas in Mohawk Valley. Those "word-pictures" may now be considered out of date, and notations have been made throughout this book. I am pleased to re-introduce an entire new generation to the events that changed this small, yet beautiful valley into the place it is today.

C. L. Neely

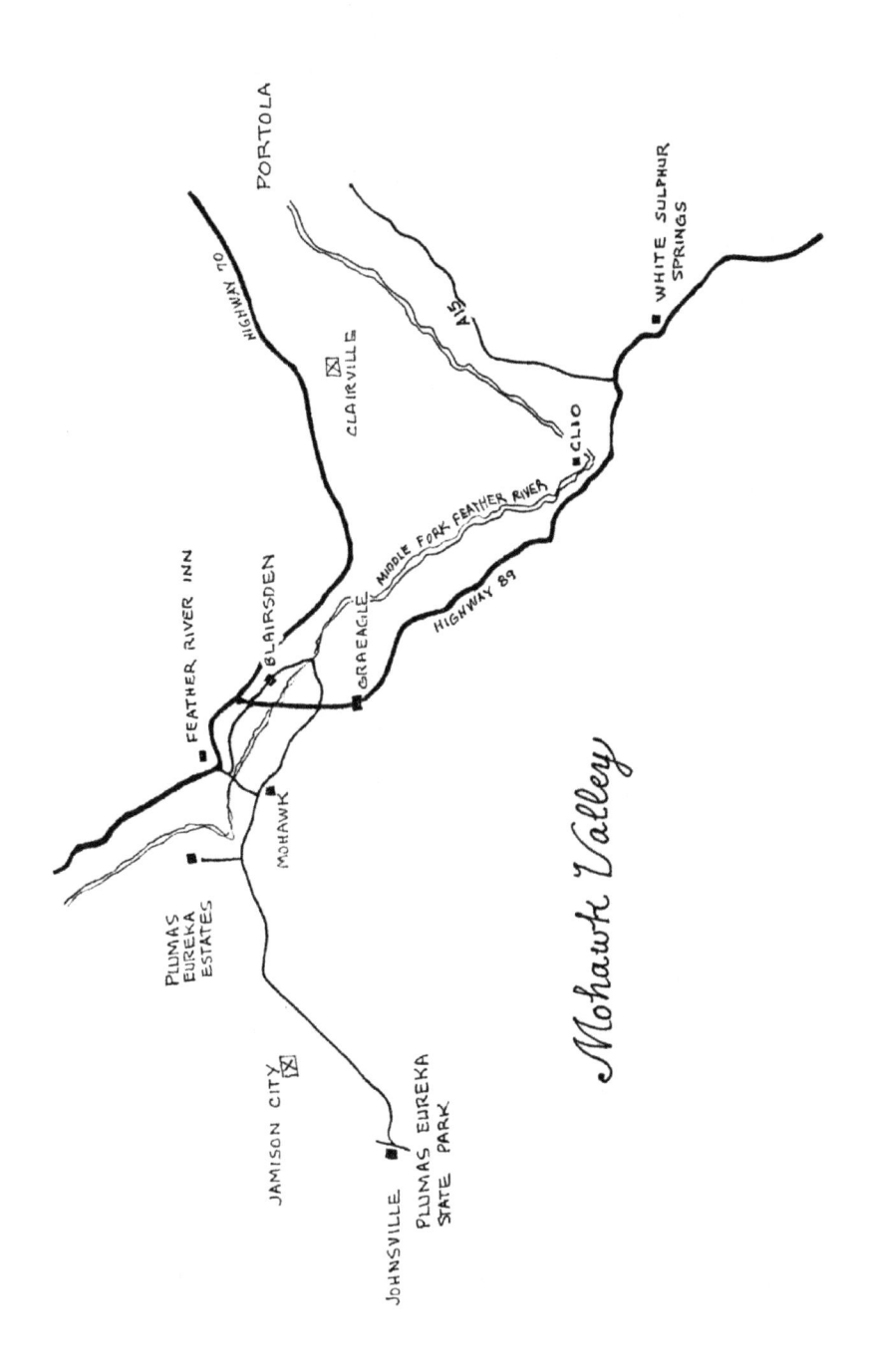

The gold rush of 1849 brought thousands of gold hungry men. They tramped up the Yuba River to Downieville and up the Feather River Canyon as far as Rich Bar. These two gold towns became the springboards for the discovery of new fertile farmlands, as discouraged miners searched the surrounding mountains for new outlets of quartz bearing gold.

Asa Gould was one of these men, and his two partners, Jamison and Friend (whose first names have been forgotten with the passing of time). They were simple rugged miners, with the glint of treasure in their eyes; and what they stumbled on in their search, was the south end of a long, green meadow land.

Asa Gould was the first to mark a claim, choosing the bank of a deep, dark river, which wound silently along the slope of a steep mountain. This uncharted water, the men later learned, was the middle fork of the Rio De Las Plumas, or Feather River. The location Gould chose is known as Clio.

Sheltered by tall pines, a short distance south of Gould's claim, the men investigated a rising cloud of steam and found a natural hot spring. Although the water reeked with a strong sulphur odor, Mr. Friend was fascinated. He claimed the location and with the help of his two partners, he built a ranch on the spot (now known as White Sulphur Springs).

Surrounded by tall mountains, the natural beauty of this valley stirred memories of their home in the Alleghenys, where they had tramped a similar plane; they began to call their new home by the same name: Mohawk Valley.

Eureka Peak, once called Gold Mountain, beckoned Jamison to leave Mohawk Valley and climb to its peak in search of gold.

JOHNSVILLE

While Gould prospected, and Friend built up his new ranch, Jamison rode his horse from one end of their newly discovered valley to the other—unsuccessfully searching for traces of gold. Could it be that on one of these outings, Jamison observed the picturesque mountain toward the west. One can almost imagine its rocky dome beckoning him to climb to its lofty peak—which he most likely did. What he would have discovered there was a group of nine prospectors, hard at work, digging out glittering quartz rocks traced with gold. A large area of the mountain had already been claimed.

If Jamison, in his search for gold, had arrived a month earlier the discovery could have been his, for that was when the nine men discovered a large, gold bearing, quartz ledge. When they realized the wealth within their reach, they each invited some friends to join them. Soon there were 36 miners chiseling away at the base of Gold

Mountain (Eureka Peak). These exuberant miners named themselves Eureka Company.

Word of a big strike filtered through the mountains like a gust of wind, and soon the surrounding forests vibrated with anxious fortune seekers. These newcomers gathered around one of the few flat area found on the east side of the steep ridge, and they created a small tent village, which they named Washington. It was not as comfortable as the new home of the Eureka Company, which was located around a small lake (Eureka Lake).

A rapid-flowing stream which ran through the town of Washington, suggests to this day that a man named Jamison was one of the first to locate in the area, as it bears the Jamison Creek. What an interesting possibility to think it may have been the same man who helped discover the hot springs.

Johnsville was once filled with large hotels and houses like this one, shown around the turn of the century.

The enormous stamp mill was so expensive to build, that it put many mines out of business.

The number of vigorous Washingtonians grew to the sum of 76. These productive men decided to combine their resources to build a 16-stamp mill to crush the gold from the quartz. They moved their village to the location of the stamp mill, and changed its name to City of 76. This new stamp mill operation cost the miners nearly $100,000. The staggering total discouraged even the most avid gambler in the group, and before a profit could be seen, they quit.

One by one, the residents of City of 76 dwindled off

and the name was inappropriate. The remnant took on a third name, that of the adjoining creek—Jamison City. On November 19, 1880, a fire ravaged the town; leaving it in ashes. The determined miners rebuilt their community however and within two years they proudly displayed a new hotel, post office, store, express office and saloon.

An interesting sideline to the history of this small village is the fact that one of their more well-known residents was a Doctor Geiger, for whom Geiger Grade (near Virginia City, NV) was named.

The Plumas Eureka Mine's bunkhouse is now a museum filled with memorabilia from Johnsville's past.

Outcroppings of other villages sprang up around the edge of Eureka Peak. Forty men established "Rough and Ready", on the south east side; and another eighty men began a place called Mammoth Company. Stamp Mills seemed to be the answer to the problem of crushing the gold from the quartz rock, and both of these two new mines built 12-stamp mills. The cost again, was immense, and the disgruntled miners quit, as early as 1854.

Eureka Company seemed blessed with good luck, from its first day, and it was the only mine successful with stamp mills. In 1855, they built a 16-stamp mill, adding eight more stamps in 1870.

A trip to Plumas Eureka State Park Museum in Johnsville will satisfy the curiosity of anyone interested in the excavations that took place on Eureka Peak.

On the side of the mountain, the park has reconstructed an actual stamp mill—authentic in its enormous size. They also have a small scale working model inside the museum, showing a stamp mill operation.

The British "invaded" Eureka Peak in 1872, when the English-owned Sierra Buttes Mining Company purchased one claim after another, until it held title on all of the quartz locations on the mountain. Apparently, the company made a slight change in the name, calling it Plumas Eureka Mine.

Ten years later, in 1882, the post office of Eureka Mills was opened, giving birth to a new town. A fellow named John Banks built a hotel there on 20 acres. He soon sold out to three English brothers, Matthew, Henry and John Willoughby. These industrious young men realized they could make a fine living by going into business—an occupation with fewer hazards, and a longer life expectancy than the mines. Together they built a merchandise store and a butcher shop.

No gold town was complete without a saloon or two so, of course, the thirsty miners welcomed German born Henry Grazer when he built a brewery. The success of this enterprise spoke for itself, when a landslide swept the brewery down the mountainside and Grazer wasted no time in rebuilding.

With gold pulled from beneath its roots, Eureka Mills produced three mercantile stores, two hotels, two meat markets, several saloons, and a school which met in a private home.

As a reminder of days gone by, the old fire hall sat peaceably alongside the Iron Door in Johnsville, before steps were made to preserve many of the old buildings.

In every town, there is one person who stands out because of his popularity. William Johns, the superintendent of Plumas Eureka Mine, was such a man. He was so well liked by his neighbors in Eureka Mills, that they changed the name of their town to honor him, and called it Johnsville.

As Johnsville grew, Jamison City shriveled, and nothing remains today to remind us of this later city. Yet, high on the mountain, Johnsville remains, in the same historic location, undisturbed by the hustle of the modern world. Attempts to preserve what is left of the few original buildings have been successful, despite treacherous winters that bury the dwellings to their rafters in snow. One of these early structures still standing is St. John's Catholic Church, nestled beside the interesting and historic Johnsville Cemetery.

Bertha Miller photo

Heavy snow fall is common to Johnsville. This photo was taken in the late 1950s'

Plumas Eureka Mine quit operations in 1943. At its peak, between 1870 and 1890, an estimated $80,000,000 in gold was extracted. The State of California established a park at the mine site in 1959. In addition to the restored stamp mill, and museum it offers a fine campground, and various out-of-doors entertainment worth investigation.

The outdoor fireplace that was used for many years by Mohawk Tavern, marks the location of the Robert Penman homestead.

MOHAWK

The mining that took place on Eureka Peak most likely had an influence on the settlement of Mohawk Valley. In 1854 (approximately two years after Jamison left the Hot springs in search for gold), two brothers named Penman settled in the northern corner of the valley. Four years earlier, they left England, crossed the Atlantic Ocean, the New England states, the vast prairies, barely passable Rocky Mountains, and Indian Territory. They were true pioneers who brought with them wives, who gave birth to children on the long journey. The Penmans were anxiously searching for new beginnings when they happily settled here. The men worked in the mines at the top of the mountain, while they stretched the hours of the days to establish farms in the valley below.

George and Sarah Penman built a log cabin where the Feather River Inn now stands; Robert and Mary Ann Penman built their house across the river. An outdoor fireplace (part of the recreational facilities of the old Mohawk Tavern) sits almost forgotten at the location of Robert Penman's homestead.

Their first neighbor, George Woodward, was also from England. He arrived in 1855, and built a sawmill at the base of the mountain near the bank of the Feather River. In 1990, the remains of an old Chevron Gas station were still visible at this site (located at the west corner of the junction of Johnsville Road, and the shortcut that leads to Mohawk Ranger Station). Woodward built a home near the mill, northeast of the junction.

Old cabins on the north end of Mohawk Valley.

Mary Ann Penman had a sister, Martha who also decided to travel to America. She left England with her family in 1857. Tragedy struck during the long journey when both her husband and her only child became very sick and died before they reached their destination. The Penmans opened their hearts to the grieving widow, and brought her to their home in Mohawk Valley. As time decreased the pain of her loss, Martha became acquainted with her new neighbor, George Woodward, and the two eventually married. This romantic alliance tied the Penmans and the Woodwards in a family bond. The two brother-in-laws became partners in the Woodward Mill. Robert Penman later operated a stage line between Jamison City and Truckee.

The northern end of Mohawk Valley increased in population very slowly, as more settlers took up land and developed farms in the area. In 1881, John B. Sutton bought the Robert Penman homestead, and built a hotel on the property. Another newcomer, William Knott, established a post office there and named it Mohawk. One year later, the new little town had its first general store.

WHITE SULPHUR SPRINGS

Several years earlier (1858 to be exact), on the south end of the valley, Fred King bought the Sulphur Springs property that Mr. Friend had settled a few years earlier. King built a hotel on the property, alongside one of the early roads connecting Jamison City with Sierra Valley, and the perfect location for a stage stop. This Sulphur Springs ranch was sold to George McLear in 1867. The new owner envisioned a summer resort and began to improve the hotel. His dream became a reality in 1871, and he advertised one of the finest hotels and resorts in the area—featuring a bath house, filled from the natural hot spring, with temperatures ranging from 72-84 degrees.

McLear also farmed his acreage, and sold produce and dairy products to the mines—like many of his neighbors were doing. He was elected Plumas County Supervisor in 1878, holding that position until 1881.

When George McLear died in 1890, the ranch was passed on to his four children. By this time, the original name of Sulphur Springs was forgotten, and throughout the county it was called McLear's. None of the McLear children had families of their own, and each one passed away without leaving an heir. The final McLear owner was George's daughter, Isabel

If George McLear sat on his veranda in the early 1880s and looked across the valley, he would have seen the ranch of his neighbor, John McKenzie (later known as Mohawk Valley Guest Ranch). Of the nine McKenzie children raised on this ranch, Mava was the one who became a good friend of Isabel McLear. And, when Isabel reached an advanced age, Mava cared for her. When Isabel died in 1950, she left the ranch to her dear friend, who also was in her declining years. When Mava died 1974, the ranch was deeded to her nephew, Harry McKenzie.

Harry and his wife Lea loved that old ranch, and under their ownership, it was completely restored and furnished with antiques and memorabilia from those days gone by, when George McLear was proprietor. Harry has since passed on, but McLear's (now known as White Sulphur Springs) still remains in the McKenzie family. It is open to the public as a Bed & Breakfast—genuine in its historical interest. The hot springs swimming pool is available for public use, but for large parties only, on a reservation basis.

NOTE: 2011 update – Since first publication of this book, White Sulphur Springs, after being vacant for several years, has deteriorated and restoration has been taken over by the Mohawk Valley Stewardship Council.

Clio in the early days   (from the Ed White Collection)

CLIO

The piece of land that Asa Gould claimed, along the Feather River, also grew in population, and by 1881 had become a small village nestled around a popular ranch run by Rebecca King. The taxpayers chose to build a bridge at this location, costing them $3,877. This little corner of the valley established its own post office and tagged it with the name Wash to honor a popular bachelor in the area.

Sometime around the turn of the century, the town of Wash lost its identity. Maybe it came with the influx of railroad construction workers, or mill hands from a fairly large sawmill in the vicinity. Whatever the reason, fourteen saloons were built in Wash, and the locals began referring to their home as "New Town", "New Mohawk" and "Boozeville". This name outraged the more conservative of the citizens who were trying to bring a school, and civilized behavior into the area. Gathering at the local store, warming themselves around the old wood stove, these residents tried to think of a more suitable name for their town. Someone's attention was drawn to the brand name printed in raised letters, on the stove: CLIO.

Located beside the gently flowing Feather River, Clio is far from a ghost town today. The warmth felt by those gathered around the wood stove many years ago still lingers. It is a one-store town, with a post office, private residences and an RV park. The friendly small-town spirit seduces summer visitors, whose curiosity takes them off the beaten path. These "snowbirds" return year after year, to enjoy the quiet charm of this area.

The main street of Clio sometime after 1903. The old railroad depot is on the right. (from the Ed White collection.)

Clairville Mill   (from the Ed White collection)

CLAIRVILLE

Just as the railroad changed the description and personality of Wash (Clio), it shifted the direction of the rest of Mohawk Valley. In 1874, the right-of-way was given to construct a new railroad from Sierra Valley (near the Nevada border) to Mohawk Valley, which was rich in farm products and timber. One can only imagine the anticipation felt by those in the valley—and their disappointment, when several years passed and the dream was not fulfilled. Twenty years later, the rails had been laid only *half* of the distance between Beckwirth (Beckwourth) and Mohawk Valley.

Henry Bowen, the owner of the Sierra Valley-Mohawk Railroad, laid out a town site near the Lloyd Bros. Mill, in a flat area where the tracks ended. He named the new community Clairville, after one of his daughters, Clair. A stage picked up passengers from this location and transported them on to Quincy, via Mohawk Valley. Within a year (in1896), a new lumber mill was constructed at Clairville, and when the rails were finally extended down the canyon to Clio (Sometime in 1902), Clairville was able to stand on its own. This male-oriented railroad and mill town constructed a roundhouse, a large hotel, a school, a Chinatown (which burned down in 1903, by an opium smoking resident), and a well-established red light district. Ten years later, Clairville was totally deserted, and nothing remains of this ghost town today.

In 1959 Blairsden was the site chosen for one of the scenes in the movie "Guns of the Timberland". The Blairsden Depot sign was replaced and it became "Deepwell" during the film making.

BLAIRSDEN

The Nevada-California-Oregon Railroad purchased the railway in 1902, the same year the tracks reached Clio. However, it would still be a few years before the construction was completed to the northern end of Mohawk Valley. Slowly the tracks crept along the same general route as the course of the Feather River. The birth of the Western Pacific Railroad (W. P.), in June 1903, put lightening in the rails, and the building of tracks took on new speed when the W. P. took over the line.

When constructing a new railroad, the builders chose certain points along the line as centers where stores and hotels would be built for the sudden impact of construction workers. The country home of James A.

Blair (one of the financiers of the W. P.) was chosen as one of these locations. As the rails drew closer to the north end of the valley, the town of Blairsden was born.

FEATHER RIVER INN

With the arrival of the railroad, growth was inevitable, and fortune was only bound by one's imagination. In 1914, the Van Noy Inter-State company purchased the land George Penman had settled on years earlier. Using giant timbers found on the property, and with an investment of $350,000, they constructed a lodge of magnificent proportions.

In a semi-circle, along the edge of the mountain they built several chalets, connected by elevated wooden walkways—which were lighted at night by electricity! The cottages varied in size some as small as four rooms, and some containing as many as twenty. Modern was the word of the day. Each cottage was furnished with showers or tubs, sun porches, and expensive furniture—even the blankets and mattresses were the best money could buy. The owners named this playground-for-the-wealthy, the Feather River Inn.

Guests of the Inn were served meals in the lodge's large dining room, with milk and butter from the resort's own dairy, and fresh vegetables and poultry raised on the resort's own farm. After breakfast, they could play tennis, or handball, practice golf at one of the putting greens, or swim in the 60x150 foot, heated swimming pool. There were card rooms, billiard rooms, reading and music rooms, and even a bowling alley. Saddle horses were available for trail riding; and for the fisherman, excellent fishing streams trickled throughout the area. If he came unprepared to fish, equipment was supplied. Hunters found an abundance of dove, mountain quail, and grouse; and deer hunters had a two month season, with a limit of two bucks, with the lodge providing a guide if requested.

Some of the chalets of the old Feather River Inn.

In the evenings, after a fun-filled day, guests were entertained with dancing in the pavilion, porch parties, or a movie in the Playhouse.

The year following the opening of the Feather River Inn, the Western Pacific Railroad introduced its passenger train—the famous California Zephyr. The Inn built a small log train station for the convenience of its guests. Years later, when the station was no longer being used, it was moved from its location beside the tracks to a spot a few hundred yards south, and was occupied for many years by the Mohawk Ranger station.

Albert Favetto bought the Inn in 1957. His experience in management, ranged from well known resorts in Switzerland to Buenos Aires. The golf course was in full use at this time, with a golf pro and gift shop. To the existing benefits, the new owner added: a resident physician, a hostess for social events, story reading for children, a Sunday morning religious service in the auditorium, and facilities for conventions.

It is probably a coincidence that in 1970, the year the California Zephyr made its last trip through the Feather River Canyon, Fayetto retired, and transferred ownership of the Inn to the Tahoe-Sierra School. The estate was then rearranged to provide services for 100 students.

The University of Pacific took ownership of the Inn in 1977. They used the school as a residential preparatory school, for approximately 10 years under the name Feather River Prep School. Recently they re-evaluated the property, and now (1990) use the Inn as a convention center, while attempts are made to improve many of the chalets and the Inn itself.

GRAEAGLE

The most well know town in all of Mohawk Valley is the town of Graeagle. Its history actually began several miles southeast, in Stampede Valley (near Truckee, California), along the bank of Davies Creek. It was there that Arthur Davies built a saw mill, in 1907. This man's interest in the lumber business was the spark that started a chain of events that transformed Mohawk Valley into the recreational playground it is today.

After 10 years of successful milling at Stampede, Davies either purchased a small existing mill, or built a second mill, in Mohawk Valley—which he named Davies Mill, just as the first one. In 1921, he sold the property to the California Fruit Exchange (CFE). The new owners ran the mill for the next 25 years, under the name Graeagle Lumber Company. The only reference to where this name came from, is attributed to Edward Baker: the Gray Eagle of the Republicans, who came through the area during its infancy, on a political campaign, and left his "reputation" attached to one of the rapid flowing streams.

Over the same railroad spur they built to carry out lumber, the CFE transported 92 house halves into its new Mohawk Valley property. The buildings were put back together, and seams can still be seen on the outside of some of the original houses. They are easily recognized where they face outward toward State Route 89, identical in color—barn red, trimmed in white. These houses were rented to employees only, who paid $15 a month, which included steam heat piped into their homes from a central plant.

The mill was a lumber mill, molding mill, and box factory. It employed about 250 men at its peak, and turned out 100,000 board feet of molding, high grade lumber, and box stock every day.

Graeagle Lumber Company was indeed a company town. It had its own slaughter house; and it had a dairy

The rock dairy of the California Fruit Exchange had showers for the milkmen.

that provided hot and cold running water, with showers for the milkmen. This unique stone building still stands on the old road to Blairsden, and still bears the California Fruit Exchange sign above its door (1990).

The company even provided entertainment for its employees, in a large community Center, where it also held dances and Christmas parties for the families.

The mill town of Graeagle had its own personality, one that blended with the lifestyle of its residents. The Graeagle Sportsmen's Club was popular with the men, especially when they sponsored local prize fights. However the most unusual event was the yearly arrival of a train load of grapes, cheered by the mass of Italian employees as it came into view on the narrow gauge railroad. Unbelievable as it may sound, the mill closed down long enough for the men to make their wine!

How old does one have to be to remember the strong wooden boxes used to ship fruit to all the local grocers? The inevitable passing of time, and progress, introduced the cardboard box. With it came an end to an era, and an end to mills like the one at Graeagle. In 1958, seven thousand acres went on the auction block. Two thousand acres of this land was developed. The sole purchaser was Harvey West & Sons, of Placerville, California.

With West's farsightedness and a little inspiration, Graeagle took on a new form and personality. Through subdividing and selling property, a planned recreational community developed from the skeleton of the company town, and the result is the highly successful tourist and retirement village that is found today.

Part of the old Graeagle Mill – 1957

The name Graeagle and Mohawk Valley naturally suggest an Indian theme. When the plans for the town were drawn, each street was given an Indian tribal name. Today the idea that Indians played a major role in the history of the area is widely accepted, and it is emphasized with totem poles and a large sign with the words "Chief Graeagle Welcomes You".

In centuries past, Mohawk Valley was a summer residence of the Maidu Indians; and Indian arrowheads can be found in all corners of the valley, but the only Chief Graeagle know to the area was from the Republican party.

The Indian theme may not be genuine, but the pride of the residents is true. Between the years of 1978 and 1981, there was a waiting list for home sites in the rapidly growing town.

Graeagle provides visitors and residents with a variety of recreational options, including horseback riding, tennis, an 18 hole golf course, and a park built around the old mill pond, which is occupied all summer with swimmers and sun bathers.

MOHAWK VALLEY'S FUTURE

Although Mohawk Valley's history may not be as romantic as it should be, it is still in the process of becoming. The newest real estate development was once a small group of summer cottages gathered together beside the Feather River a short distance off of the Johnsville road. In a few short years, this quiet little nook, which for years was called Lundy's (for the owner of much of the property, Colonel Lundy), was transformed into another expensive planned community, under the name of Plumas Eureka Estates—complete with condominiums and an 18 hole golf course.

Plans are also on the drawing board (1990) for a third planned recreational community in Mohawk Valley, to be located on the south end at the old McKenzie Ranch, later known as Mohawk Valley Guest Ranch, and now called Whitehawk Ranch.

What began as fertile farm land, where crops were grown for the benefit of gold mines, may see a future as a playground for the rich and famous. The quiet, gentle beauty, enjoyed by generations past, is quickly disappearing, and this day may soon be written down in history as "one of the good old days"!

END

More Pictures of Mohawk Valley

The railroad trestle near Clio - 1977

The Western Pacific Hotel in Clio

Raised walkways at the Feather River Inn

This barn was part of the Feather River Inn facilities.

Mohawk Valley in the 1920s

View of Johnsville seated in its basin at the foot of Eureka Peak.

Bertha Miller photo

Clio Post Office 1958

A favorite summer pastime in the 1980 was diving off the Graeagle Millpond Dam.

BIBLIOGRAPHY

- Brown, Ed. "The Penmans: Looking to Plumas County's Past History." <u>Portola Reporter</u>, October 23, 1985, p. 8B
- Buck, Jan. "Feather River Inn." <u>Sierra Booster</u>, October 5, 1984, pp. 12, 13.
- "Clairville Memories," <u>Portola Reporter</u>, June 5, 1975, pp. 6, 7.
- Dunn, Mary E. (Phelps). <u>What's in a Name?</u> Historical Society Pub. No. 1 (Quincy: Plumas County Historical Society, September 11, 1960).
- Fariss & Smith. <u>History of Plumas, Lassen, a& Sierra Counties,</u> Fariss & Smith, 1882
- "Graeagle as a Mill town," <u>Portola Reporter</u>, April 26, 1979 Gubel, Sandra.
- "Graeagle: Former Mill town Becomes Retirement Haven." <u>Portola Reporter</u>, September 4, 1985, p. 9
- Hall, Helen: "Clio Excavation Reveals Possible Prehistoric Camp." <u>Portola Reporter,</u> September 18, 1985
- "Historic Johnsville Church Not Forgotten." <u>Portola Reporter,</u> April 30, 1986, p. 2A
- "Mohawk Valley Ranch Comes to Life." <u>Portola Reporter</u>, May 29, 1985, p. 7A
- Myrick, David F. <u>Railroads of Nevada and Eastern California.</u> Vol. I of <u>The Northern Roads.</u> Berkley: Howell-North books, 1962
- <u>Plumas-Eureka State Park.</u> Sacramento: Department of Parks and Recreation.
- "What's in a name? – Plumas: How Places Were Named." <u>Portola Reporter</u>, February 5, 1986, p. 9A.

NOTES:

About the Author

C. L. Neely is a native of Northern California and lived for several years in Mohawk Valley, near White Sulphur Springs. Interest in the local history began at an early age and Neely's love for books led to the ownership of three bookstores, and the publication of a book on the history of Sierra Valley, titled *Behind Every Hero* which was an accumulation of fifteen years of research on the historical details of Sierra County. Cartooning is another love of the author who has illustrated two cookbooks, a magazine article, designed dozens of greeting cards under the Chicken Scratch logo, and was a partner is a sweatshirt design company named 5th Sparrow. C. L. Neely is married with four children and ten grandchildren and is now retired and lives in Oregon.

Other books by C. L. Neely:
Behind Every Hero

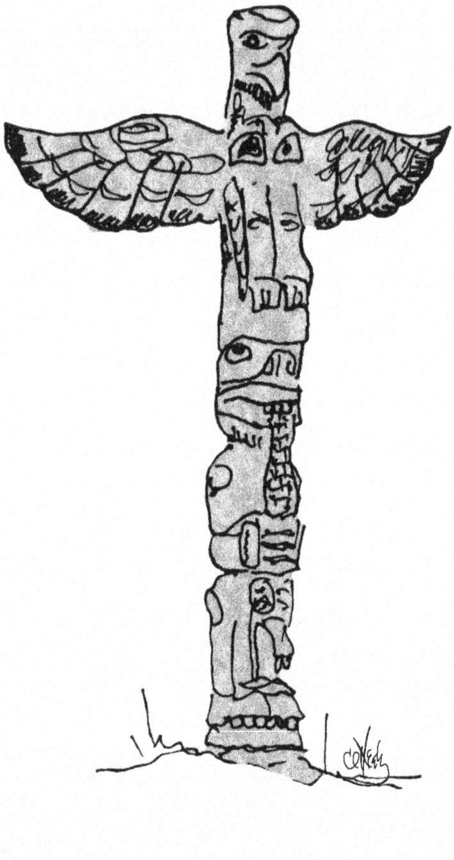

CPSIA information can be obtained
at www.ICGtesting.com
Printed in the USA
LVHW051325101218
599884LV00005B/640/P